PLANNING

Ahead For Those You Love

Trusted Advice From A Skilled
Estate Planning Lawyer

Nicholas A. Giuditta III,
Attorney at Law

Jacobs & Whitehall
9600 Escarpment Blvd
Suite 745-282
Austin, TX 78749
(888) 570-7338
www.jacobsandwhitehall.com

Ordering Information:

Quantity sales. Special discounts are available on quantity purchases by corporations, associations, and others. For details, contact the publisher at the address above.

Orders by U.S. trade bookstores and wholesalers. Please contact Jacobs & Whitehall: Tel: (888) 570-7338 or visit www.jacobsandwhitehall.com.

Printed in the United States of America

Published in 2023

ISBN: 978-1-954506-78-7

PREFACE

When I decided to devote my career to estate planning law, there was a simple reason. I wanted to advise people about the significance of having their affairs in order. Too often, I have seen people pass away without Wills and the chaos that can cause their heirs ranging from disputes about who owns real estate to the person who will be appointed as estate representative. Similarly, people who have not prepared Powers of Attorney and became ill, then needed their adult child to go through the lengthy, complicated and otherwise unnecessary guardianship process.

Helping people plan for the future and ensuring an orderly transfer of their assets motivates me on a daily basis. I am privileged to represent so many people in my area and assist them in this goal.

Many books on estate planning are designed for lawyers, law students and academics. That is not this book. Instead, this book is written with you, the individual lay person, in mind. I want you to understand the importance of estate planning to yourself and your family.

I hope this book provides you valuable and practical information that will allow you to make good estate planning decisions for you and your heirs.

DEDICATION

I dedicate this book to the memory of my parents, Nicholas and Linda Giuditta, who taught me the values of persistence and hard work at a young age. This has served me well in my life's work as an estate planning lawyer. I also dedicate this book to my loving wife Francine and our two sons, Nicholas and Christopher.

DISCLAIMER

This publication is intended to be used for educational purposes only. No legal advice is being given, and no attorney-client relationship is intended to be created by reading this material. The author assumes no liability for any errors or omissions or for how this book or its contents are used or interpreted, or for any consequences resulting directly or indirectly from the use of this book. For legal or any other advice, please consult an experienced attorney or the appropriate expert, who is aware of the specific facts of your case and is knowledgeable in the law in your jurisdiction.

Giuditta Law

141 Elmer Street

Westfield, NJ 07090

www.giudittalaw.com

(908) 232-0099

TESTIMONIALS

"Nick is top notch. I've known him since law school, and even though I am an attorney, I needed Nick's expertise in assisting with my parents' situation, which involved dementia and other myriad issues. Nick is calm and reassuring, and knew exactly how to handle such a complex and emotional situation. He was patient and listened. He provided excellent advice and was incredibly attentive. He is knowledgeable, proficient and responsive. And I can tell you that mine was a very unusual situation, and Nick stepped up to the plate and handled everything with confidence, class, and elan. I never hesitate to recommend him to anyone needing assistance in estate planning."

– Kathleen Dooley

(General Counsel, Hu-manity.co)

****

"I had no idea estate planning was so important until my mom was diagnosed with cancer and had 6 weeks to live. A neighbor recommended Nicholas Giuditta. The first phone call and meeting sealed the deal. His compassion, understanding, and willingness to guide me thru this process when time was of the essence lifted a large burden off of my shoulders. Estate planning at any time is overwhelming but Nick was there with professional guidance and a shoulder to lean on every step of the way. He was always willing to answer any questions, give legal advice, and assist in handling a lot of family drama. I was so pleased with Nick's services, that my husband and I actually did 'our' estate planning with Nick. I would highly recommend Nicholas Giuditta! You not only receive the best professional help but also make a friend in the process!"

– Michele ONeil

****

"I hired Nick Giuditta to settle legal issues regarding my mother's estate. I found him to be a very knowledgeable and capable attorney who carefully listened to the problems about my mother's estate, asked questions, and he took the time to explain my options and the pros and cons of each possible outcome. I also found him to be always professional, diligent, efficient and transparent in keeping me informed as to everything he was working on that led to the ultimate goal of fairly settling all of the legal issues on my mother's estate. He met and exceeded all of my expectations. I would hire him again to represent me, and I would not hesitate to recommend Nick's legal talents, skills and abilities to any person."

– Peter Strozniak

****

"I hired Mr. Giuditta to handle my late father's estate. He did an excellent job in explaining to me what the legalities were concerning my father's last will and testament. There were items he pointed out that I didn't even realize I was entitled to that brought upon a messy lawsuit by my family. Mr. Giuditta represented me throughout the proceedings with professionalism and dignity. The outcome was favorable for both sides but sadly proved that money is the root to all evil. I would hire him again without question."

– Rich Parrillo

****

"Nick Giuditta was there during the worst days of my life. It's not often when you come across a lawyer who really cares. He was instrumental in settling my father's estate. His guidance is what I had hoped for. He effectively communicated each step that needed to be taken and made certain I had a clear understanding of the process. He is empathetic towards his clients' needs and also builds a strong rapport with those he interacts with. I would highly recommend Nick to anyone who is searching for a lawyer."

– Susan

****

"I was referred to Nicholas Giuditta by a friend to have some legal documents drawn up. Mr. Giuditta was very professional, explaining the purpose and use of each and every document, listening to my questions and input. I found him to be very understanding and pleasant to deal with. I would certainly use him for other similar matters and would highly recommend him to others."

– Jon Chisholm

****

"I've engaged Nick on a couple of separate occasions where I was appointed as executor. Nick was very knowledgeable on all issues I've had to deal with including liquidation of private investments. I've even used Nick for my own estate planning."

– Robert Lopez

Chief Financial Officer, Crystal Review, LLC

****

TABLE OF CONTENTS

i.	**Preface**	**3**
ii.	**Dedication**	**5**
iii.	**Testimonials**	**7**
iv.	**About The Author**	**14**
1.	**Common Misconceptions**	**19**
2.	**The Goal Of Proper Estate Planning**	**26**
3.	**The Problems With Not Planning Ahead**	**34**
4.	**The Timing Factor**	**38**
5.	**Diving Deeper Into Wills**	**45**
6.	**Estate Planning Tools To Protect Your Assets And Your Loved Ones**	**51**

7. **Health Care Documents And Naming Decision Makers** **55**

8. **Adult Guardianships** **60**

9. **Additional Advantages Of Estate Planning** **65**

10. **Probate** **69**

11. **The Difference The Right Firm Makes** **74**

v. **What Is The Next Step?** **78**

vi. **Index** **79**

vii. **Notes** **82**

About The Author

How I Started Trusts And Estates Work

I've been practicing law for 35 years. I wanted to be a lawyer since I was a freshman in college, and I always aspired to have my own practice. So in 2000, I opened my own firm in Cranford, New Jersey, a town a couple of miles from Westfield.

I was a self-starter and taught myself trust & estate law. I used to be primarily a litigation attorney in the 1990's though I always wanted to practice trust and estate (T&E) work as I viewed it as a way to help people and solve problems.

So, I went to many seminars and practiced in a building with another T&E lawyer. Eventually, I began to give seminars to the public, initially on the importance of wills, powers of attorney, and advance directives. As the years went by, I became known to my colleagues, clients, and others as someone that does lots of trust and estate work, including planning, probate, and select estate litigation cases.

My Law Journey And Background

Out of law school, I started as an assistant prosecutor after clerking for a judge. I was with a small firm for about seven years doing primarily insurance defense. I left that firm to start my own trust and estate practice. At this point in my experience, I've written over a thousand wills for my clients. We also have many probate, or estate administration clients, probably having administered hundreds of estates.

As I gained more experience with trust and estate work, I became involved in the Trusts, Estates and Elder Law Committee of the Union County Bar Association. In 2010, I joined the Union County Trusts Estates and Elder Law Committee as a co-chair, and am also a trustee and officer of the Union County Bar Association, where I am presently the Secretary.

I started to give seminars to other lawyers both within the county bar and also at the state bar, through the Institute for Continuing Legal Education. Now, we're giving seminars to professionals in this area as well. Our seminars have covered a variety of topics over the years. For example, we have lectured on New Jersey's estate tax (which was abolished in 2018) and how writings can be intended as wills if they're not prepared formally.

I receive referrals from the court system. This may be to serve as administrator of estates when people die without wills, or to represent the interests of incapacitated persons in guardianship proceedings. Many of my referrals, particularly in the last few years, have come from other lawyers who don't have as much knowledge about trust and estate law.

I'm very involved with the county bar and with giving seminars to laypeople and fellow lawyers – recently and prior to the COVID-19 pandemic. I also used to be very involved in local politics. I was on the Town Council of Cranford in the late 90s, and was also deputy mayor.

There are many similarities between politics and being a lawyer, in terms of solving problems and dealing with different personalities and issues, and these experiences helped me learn how to get along with different types of individuals and satisfy constituent or client needs.

The Biggest Key Takeaways For Readers

Of course, I hope readers learn a lot from this book, but the biggest takeaway is how incredibly important it is to have these three critical documents in New Jersey:

- The will;
- The power of attorney; and
- The advance directive.

It's so easy to avoid the problems that come about when you don't have these pillars of estate planning in place – just by taking the time to create them.

Additionally, I hope this book impresses upon my readers the significance of visiting the right professional to get these documents done correctly. In my seminars, I give examples of what can happen when you don't have a will. I also discuss whether you need a guardianship, especially if you don't have a power of attorney.

I share all of this information because I want people to understand the significance of completing these documents correctly, as well as why they are vital, and what can happen if you don't have them.

CHAPTER 1

COMMON MISCONCEPTIONS

Misconception #1: Living Trusts Are Always Needed

One of the most common misconceptions for people in New Jersey is about the importance of living trusts.

One thing we see frequently is that people think they need a living trust when they actually don't. Sometimes people will come into my office and say, "I need a trust. I need a living trust. I heard it from Suzy Orman. Everyone needs a living trust."

The reality is, you probably only need a living trust if you live in a state where probate is very complex so that you can stay out of probate. This is in part due to the many hoops your executor must jump through with the courts - they have to file inventories and accountings, and a whole host of other things.

New York is a great example of how difficult probate is, in addition to Florida and Arizona. In these states, people create living trusts while they're alive (or they should!), and they transfer their assets out of their name into a living trust so that when they die, there is no need to go to probate - or it's at least less of a hassle. That's a very good thing in certain states, but in New Jersey, things are a little bit different.

Probate In New Jersey

People understandably hear about living trusts and they think it's something needed in New Jersey. In reality, however, good estate planning lawyers in

New Jersey mostly use wills. This is because probate is an easier process in New Jersey.

Generally, the executor brings an original death certificate and an original will to the surrogate's office, which is the office that handles these affairs in the county in which the person died.

As long as there are two witnesses and a notary on the will, the executor gets a letter of testamentary. This is the legal piece of paper that says they can now take action on behalf of the estate, usually in conjunction with their lawyer.

In New Jersey, there is usually no other involvement with the probate court or the surrogate court. There is no need to file a list of all the assets the person owned, or to get permission to sell a house.

Compared to many other states, New Jersey's probate process is not cumbersome at all. Since the probate process is easy, living trusts confer no advantage to a client in New Jersey in terms of staying out of probate.

Misconception #2: Living Trusts Have Tax Advantages

Another misconception is that a living trust provides tax advantages…

Sometimes people think, "Well, if I put everything in a living trust and I die, there are no taxes at all." But this is not true.

Because a living trust is revocable, it can be changed anytime. The law views it as if the person still owns the assets, so if there were estate or inheritance tax issues, the living trust doesn't save the person from those expenses.

Misconception #3: No Money, No Will

A very common misunderstanding people have is that if they don't have a lot of money, they don't need a will. The problem with this idea is that even if you don't have a lot, you're still creating problems for your loved ones.

For example, imagine someone has four kids who will inherit from them. Their spouse passes away, and then they pass away with no will.

In New Jersey, all four kids would have an equal right to be appointed administrator of the estate. The estate administrator is the person who makes decisions about the deceased person's assets and can take action on their behalf.

(Note: When someone dies without a will, this person is called an administrator. When someone dies with the will, they are called an executor.)

If the deceased person's children don't agree on who should be the administrator, or which two should be co-administrators, it becomes a problem. With a will, the person would have named an executor – and when an executor is named clearly, it's easy to get the will probated, and the executor can begin taking action within 30 days of their death, or sometimes even sooner.

Another issue is that even when the person has no money, they likely still have property or other assets. For instance, let's say the person in the above example has a house worth $400,000, with no mortgage – that's a big asset. However, no one can sell the asset from the estate until the four kids agree on who should be the administrator. So, how can this issue get resolved?

If the estate gets an offer to have the house purchased, because they still do not have an estate administrator, they can't sell the house. Now, the kids may be fighting over who should be the administrator.

Only the administrator can sign a deed, which transfers the property to the new owners. If the kids are fighting over who should be the administrator, then they lose out on the ability to sell the estate house. Then, the market goes down a little, so they stop fighting, appoint an administrator, and sell the house, but it is for $50,000 less.

This is a good example of why you need a will, even if you don't have much money. Even if you didn't have a house, if you have $30,000 in stock, that stock can't be transferred to the beneficiaries unless there is an estate representative.

You cannot get an estate representative seamlessly appointed without a will. You have to jump through more hoops, even when people agree on who should be the administrator. It takes more time to get the estate representative appointed when you die without a will.

This idea that you only need a will if you have a lot of assets is definitely false. You cannot get anything done in an estate unless there's a representative appointed. The simplest way to have a representative appointed quickly is to name the person in the will, and then it's done.

Planning Ahead For Those You Love

Most people don't want to talk about death or planning for death, which is understandable. But it's important, because dying without a will creates a lot of problems that don't need to be there and makes things unnecessarily complicated. In creating a will and planning ahead, you're making it easier for your loved ones to deal with and accomplish things after you pass.

CHAPTER 2

THE GOAL OF PROPER ESTATE PLANNING

The Main Estate Planning Documents

When most lawyers are talking about estate planning, we are in essence talking about three documents:

1. A will;
2. A power of attorney; and
3. An advance directive.

Each of these documents has a specific purpose…

The Will

The goal of a will is to clearly state who is inheriting your estate, and what percentage of your estate or which pieces of your estate they should receive. This includes real estate, stocks, and other assets. The will should also clearly identify an estate representative so that it's easy and quick to get things accomplished on behalf of the estate.

The ultimate goal of the will is this: You want to make sure the people you intend to benefit are clearly identified, and what they receive is specified. It's essentially the "who gets what" document. This is especially important when someone does not have kids but has many extended family members, perhaps several nieces, nephews, or cousins. They may want some family members to inherit something, but not others.

In summary, the will can help get your estate in order through two main actions:

1. Identifying an estate executor; and

2. Naming your beneficiaries.

The intention of clearly identifying both the executor and the beneficiaries is that there should be no dispute about these after someone passes away.

The Power Of Attorney

The second document, the power of attorney (POA), also has multiple important purposes. Let's look at what it accomplishes…

First of all, the power of attorney appoints someone who steps into your shoes to do what you would normally do. This could be actions such as the following:

- Signing deeds
- Talking to people or signing legal documents on your behalf
- Paying your bills
- Making non-life-or-death medical decisions
- And more…

The power of attorney is very broad and can serve you in various ways. In a worst-case scenario, if you become mentally incapacitated and you've previously appointed a power of attorney, they can transact all your affairs for you.

More commonly, you may not be mentally incapacitated, but you might be mentally frail. Or you might be 100% fine mentally, but you're in the hospital for three weeks for physical ailments, and you need somebody to go out and do some things for you. (Even in this day and age, powers of attorney need to be physically present at locations to transact business for you.)

If you don't appoint a POA, this can be a real problem later down the road. For example, if you become mentally incapacitated and don’t have a POA, now you can't give anyone power of attorney because of your condition. The power of attorney is a legal document, and you cannot sign a legal document if you don't have full mental awareness.

We have seen cases like this where someone absolutely needs a decision maker. They may be in a nursing home, or they’ve become mentally incompetent, such as with conditions like advanced dementia. But because they never gave anyone the power of attorney, there's no one to make decisions for them.

So, what happens in these scenarios?

Somebody, usually a family member, has to go to court to seek a guardianship over that person to become their legal decision-maker. This could be avoided if the person who now needs a guardianship had just gone to a lawyer earlier and done a power of attorney.

A power of attorney can be completed relatively quickly, typically in a week or two. Under emergency circumstances, we can have a quick turnaround in a couple of days. It's not a very complicated document, but it can help a person and their family avoid a myriad of problems.

Avoiding A Guardianship

Having to get a guardianship is not ideal. It's very cumbersome, it's time consuming, and it's much more expensive than a power of attorney. The court must be involved, and it's a 2-to-4-month process.

We see the need for guardianships when people haven't done a POA, or sometimes when they've done an improper POA. This could occur when the documents were incomplete or of bad quality — for instance, if they pull the paperwork from online, that can be a problem.

However, the goal of the POA is to have a decision maker in place and avoid the need for a guardianship. For anyone that does a proper estate plan, their family will never have to think about guardianship, as it will be an issue that has already been addressed through the POA.

The Advance Directive

The goal of the advance directive is to clearly indicate how you want to be treated if you're in an end-of-life situation.

The advance directive applies in a scenario where there is no reasonable expectation of recovery from a serious accident or illness, based on medical science. It states whether you would want life support discontinued or not instituted. In other words, it specifies whether or not you want heroic measures taken.

The Terri Schiavo Case

The purpose of the advance directive is to have your wishes in writing, because if they're not, you could have a Terri Schiavo situation.

This was a case in Florida during the 90s when a 26-year-old woman became in a vegetative state. Her parents were still alive, and she was married. Not surprisingly, due to her young age, she did not have an advance directive.

Essentially, her husband and parents disagreed about her treatment. Her husband said, "She told me years ago that if she was ever like this, to take her off life support."

However, her parents said, "She didn't have an advance directive and there is nothing in writing. She's our daughter, and we don't want her off of life support. We want heroic measures to be taken."

Since they couldn't agree and nothing was in writing, there was a big, long court battle between her parents and her husband. Obviously, it's best to avoid this type of situation. When someone's wishes are in writing, then we don't have to rely on oral statements of what someone may or may not have said.

When you have an advance directive in writing that states your wishes, it names somebody to make the decision to continue or discontinue life support. That person is called the health care proxy. Typically, the health care proxy is a spouse, and then an adult child as an alternate.

Besides making sure your treatment wishes are followed, the advance directive helps avoid a potentially unpleasant situation among family members, who may think you have said different things over the years.

Overall, the goal of proper estate planning – short-term or long-term – is to make things easier for you and your loved ones. In most instances, that's the ultimate goal you want to accomplish with estate plans.

CHAPTER 3

THE PROBLEMS WITH NOT PLANNING AHEAD

The Consequences Of Not Having A Will In Place

When someone dies without a will in New Jersey, the New Jersey statutes decide what happens to their estate. In comparison, when you have a will, it doesn't matter what the statutes say, within reason, whatever you have stated in the will happens.

Impacts On Your Loved Ones

Not having a will can have extremely negative consequences on your family…

For example, let's say you have three children, and one of them has very serious special needs. You die without a will, and your spouse has already passed. Neither of you has written a will to properly plan for that child or created a special needs trust.

Under New Jersey law, each child would inherit equally, but if the child with special needs is on Medicaid, or receives certain other government benefits, he will likely be removed from those programs because of the inheritance. If the parents had planned properly and worked with a lawyer, the lawyer could have helped the family better protect and care for their child with special needs.

For a child on Medicaid or Supplemental Security Income (SSI) who has a condition such as cerebral palsy, we can create a special needs trust to hold the inheritance on his behalf. If it was specified in a will that the share for this child with special needs should go to the trust rather than directly to him, the child would not have been disqualified for Medicaid, or SSI, solving the family's problem.

The Bottom Line

Essentially, if you die without a will, the state determines where your money goes – not you. That's the simplest way to put it. The main reason you need estate planning in New Jersey is to make sure your assets pass the way you want them to pass.

What's more, if you have more than one child and you die without a will in New Jersey, each of your kids has an equal right to be an administrator. If they don't agree, or they take many months to figure it out, the estate may lose out on opportunities, like selling a house or transferring assets.

Posting Bond

Another thing people don't realize is that if you die without a will in New Jersey, the administrator has to post a bond. That means the estate has to pay a premium to an insurance company to ensure that the administrator does their job.

If the administrator was grossly negligent or took money from the estate, the bond would pay the other beneficiaries. This is a cumbersome process – it takes time to get a bond and it's obviously an expense to the estate. In addition, not every administrator can qualify for a bond, depending on their credit score.

This is another aspect that slows the process down, makes it more expensive, and is totally unnecessary. When we create wills in New Jersey, we always state that the executor will serve without bond, which cuts out an unnecessary process.

The purpose of a bond is to protect the estate from a potentially untrustworthy administrator. However, when you appoint your own executor, you can ensure you are choosing someone you trust to take care of your estate. In this case, a bond would not be required.

CHAPTER 4

THE TIMING FACTOR

Delaying Your Estate Planning

Talking about death and planning for after your passing can create a lot of anxiety for many people. For this reason, it's very normal for some people to put off estate planning because they don't want to talk or think about it.

However, we find that families with children are generally more proactive and usually don't put off estate planning as much as others. Why? Because it's usually fairly clear what they want to do – they want to protect and provide for their children, and they often have a good idea about who they want to manage their affairs.

The people that seem to put it off or have a hard time deciding are typically those who are older and without children. They often hold off until their sixties or seventies. Since they don't have kids, they may think it is not a big deal. What's more, sometimes they simply don't know who they want to name as beneficiaries.

If they have no kids but seven or eight nieces or nephews, the relationship between them (the testator) and the nieces and nephews is almost always different than it would be between the testator and their own children.

What commonly occurs is that the testator - the person writing the will - is not really sure what to do. Maybe they think 2 of the 7 nieces are great, but they rarely see the other nieces and nephews. They don't know them as well as they would know their own kids. Ultimately, they struggle to decide which of their relatives to list as beneficiaries, and which to leave out of their will. For a conventional nuclear family, it's usually easier to make these decisions.

The Best Time To Start Planning

Certainly, the best time to start planning is when you have kids. Even with a first baby, it's crucial to think about a guardianship for your child. But even if the best time to start planning has passed, it's almost never too late to start estate planning.

Even if you're on your deathbed, as long as you're mentally competent, you can still write a will. You can still ask yourself, "Who's going to be my executor? Who do I leave my things to?" – and put the answers to these questions in a written document.

The only time it's too late legally is if you've become mentally incapacitated. In this situation, you cannot create a will, just like you cannot appoint a power of attorney, because you would not fully understand your actions.

Guardianship Planning

In a perfect world, families with children should probably start putting an estate plan in place shortly before their first child is born. Certainly, when you have a child or two, that's a good time to start planning.

You have to remember this: If both parents die before any of their kids reach 18, the child or children will need a guardian. This is somebody who will raise them and, ideally, shares the parents' child-rearing philosophy.

If you don't name a guardian in your will, or you don't have a will, you're taking a huge risk. Most likely, people on both sides of the family will be trying to be the guardian, and it's not always in the best interest of the children.

It creates chaos, and you don't want chaos in that kind of situation. You want a will that clearly states your wishes for a guardian – this creates a situation that is much better than having four or five people going to court arguing why they should be the guardian.

Different Plans For Different Life Phases

Estate Planning is not a one-size-fits-all situation. Different phases in life can require something different. A good example of this would be a couple with three children…

When they are a young couple and their kids are all under 15, they come into our office to write a will. At that point in time, they may want to set up a trust for their children. They decide that if they both die before the kids reach 25, their assets will be held in the trust.

But after 20 years, they decide that the trust is no longer needed. Their kids are older, and they've shown that they are responsible. They decide to get rid of the trusts and leave the money directly to their children.

Also, when the couple originally did the will in their 30s, they couldn't name their kids as executors or trustees because they were under 18. Likely, the young couple would have named siblings or someone else as executors, trustees, or guardians. Now, fast-forward 20 years to when the couple is in their 50s. With the kids in their 20s or 30s, they can name their kids as executors or trustees of the trust.

At this point in their lives, it makes more sense for their children to be in these roles, so they would need to adjust their will accordingly. They should remove their siblings, who were previously appointed to these roles, and name their children as executors or trustees.

A similar scenario can occur with the advance directive. When you're a young couple, it makes the most sense to have a husband or wife named as the health care proxy. An alternate health care proxy for someone in their 30s could be their parents, or a brother or sister that you trust. But as your kids get older, you generally want them to be the alternate health care proxy – not your brother or sister.

You really don't want a situation where you're 60 and need a health care proxy, and your 68-year-old brother shows up to make this decision in the hospital with your 34-year-old daughter. With a highly personal choice whether to discontinue the life support of a parent, an adult child of 34 or 38, for example, is likely sufficiently mature enough to make that decision.

In addition, your own child is a more natural selection for the health care proxy than your 68-year-old brother. With the dynamics of that situation, it would not really make sense for a sibling of the person who made the advance directive to have the authority, as opposed to the daughter.

These are some examples of where different phases of life require different choices of fiduciaries — executors, trustees, health care proxies in the advance directive, and of course, the power of attorney.

CHAPTER 5

DIVING DEEPER INTO WILLS

The Benefits Of A Will

A will is one of three main estate planning documents, and it offers some critical protections. Here are some of the ways that a will serves you:

- You can name an executor who can act almost immediately. (In New Jersey, executors face no real time delay.)
- If you have minor children, it names guardians who can take care of your kids if both parents

die. This provides order for your kids and makes life easier for the people you leave behind.

- It names a trustee, if this is something you need.
- You can avoid the need for your loved ones to go to court to figure out who will fill these roles, which doesn't need to happen if you die without a will.

The Limitations Of A Will

A will provides important advantages, but it still has limitations…

For example, it is common for most people to have 401(k)s, and IRAs now. So if you have an IRA and you've named your two kids as beneficiaries, the will doesn't determine what happens to that IRA. In other words, the beneficiary designation you completed for the IRA determines who gets the money. (This is actually a good thing – you really don't want IRAs passing through wills for tax reasons.)

While not a negative aspect, another limitation of a will is that it doesn't dispose of the assets for which you've named beneficiaries. This applies to the relationship between a will and several other types of accounts and documents…

Wills And Certificates Of Deposits

Another limitation of a will lies in its relationship with other assets and accounts, such as certificates of deposits (CDs). Many certificates of deposit have a payable-on-death beneficiary that a will does not override.

Frequently, we see cases where people have more than one child and they have listed one of their children as the payable upon death beneficiary of their CD.

They think that because they named all of their children in their will to receive equal shares that this also applies to the CD. They think that their will trumps the payable-on-death designation and that the CD will also be split equally between their children. However, this is not the case.

The payable-on-death designation means that the asset passes outside the will. A will cannot dispose of assets that have designated beneficiaries. If you wanted those assets to pass through your will, you can't just name beneficiaries and then those assets pass through your will.

Wills And Trusts

Similarly, another limitation of a will lies in its relationship to trusts. A will cannot override the rules set up for a trust.

For instance, imagine that you transferred a piece of real estate to a trust during your lifetime. The trust document states how the real estate is going to pass when you die.

You cannot then write a will that attempts to pass the piece of real estate through the will. This is because the trust already has language in it that decides where that real estate goes.

Wills And Joint Accounts

Many people think they need to create a joint account with their child so their kid can pay their bills after they pass. However, a better option would be to give your child power of attorney so they can handle more than just paying some of your bills.

One of the problems with a joint account - in New Jersey, and probably in most states - is when someone has multiple children but a joint account with only one child.

For example, if a mother owns an account with her daughter, Jill, when the mother passes, Jill can legitimately claim the account. She can say, "I own all this joint account because I'm a joint survivor." However, the mother's will might state that everything goes to her four kids - not just Jill.

It might be possible to work it out with Jill so that she treats the account as if it should go through the will. But in some cases, you may get a child that says, "Well, I'm the surviving joint account owner. I get all of this account."

When she was creating the will, her mother thought that her will would control the joint account as well - but it doesn't. So as you can see, opening a joint account with only one of multiple children as a surviving owner can create real issues.

CHAPTER 6

ESTATE PLANNING TOOLS TO PROTECT YOUR ASSETS AND YOUR LOVED ONES

Setting Up Trusts

Setting up a trust within a will is a good estate planning tool if you're concerned about a beneficiary receiving the money directly.

A typical situation would be parents who have adolescent or young adult kids. Of course, you don't want a will that directs everything to your child if he or she is 10 years old. What would happen in this circumstance is that, because a 10-year-old cannot inherit your assets directly, a guardian account would have to be set up. This is a very cumbersome process.

A better way to plan in that situation is to specify an age when the child can inherit the funds. For example, if any of your kids are under 30, the money goes into a trust you've created in the body of the will, instead of going to them directly.

You can name a trustee who will manage the money for their benefit. The money can be used to pay for things like:

- Education
- Health
- Maintenance and support
- And more…

Then, when the child is 30, the money that is left in the trust gets distributed to them outright.

Trusts can be tremendously helpful estate planning tools, either for minors or in situations where people don't want their kids to inherit until they're a certain age. Young adults are still forming and figuring out their life. They're still young and impressionable, and this might not be the best time for them to receive an inheritance. A trust created in the will is a very good estate planning tool for that situation.

Additional Benefits Of A Trust

Trusts can also be a useful tool when parents may be concerned about the stability of their child's marriage. For instance, we frequently see parents leaving funds for their children in trusts rather than leaving the money to their children directly. The intent behind this is to ensure that only their child has access to the trust in case of a divorce, and not their child's spouse.

They may leave the money in trust for the life of their son or daughter, or sometimes until their son or daughter is 60, for example. This is more common when people have concerns about the stability of their kids' marriage.

Trusts can also be set up for adult children who may be less capable of handling money, such as if an adult child has a gambling problem. You create a trust in the will so that a trustee manages the money for the benefit of the beneficiary, rather than the child getting the money directly.

CHAPTER 7

HEALTH CARE DOCUMENTS AND NAMING DECISION MAKERS

Advance Directives

The healthcare document that we typically prepare as attorneys is the advance directive, and it contains two parts:

1. The living will. It states the person's instructions about what needs to be present in order for the health care proxy to discontinue life support.

2. The health care proxy designation. This is where you appoint somebody to speak for you to make decisions about whether to continue or discontinue life support. Typically, the health care proxy is one spouse for the other, and then a backup is an adult child.

An advance directive only comes into play if you can't communicate your own wishes. As long as you can speak for yourself, it is not applicable.

Making Decisions: Health Care Proxy vs. Power Of Attorney

The role of the health care proxy is to make decisions about end-of-life care and treatment, based on your living will. However, the power of attorney makes financial decisions. They would have access to your money and make decisions about when and how to spend your money, when necessary.

The power of attorney also has medical-related decision-making authority. For instance, picking which hospital, nursing home, or assisted living facility you should go to falls under their responsibilities.

They can take action for you relating to both finances and health care, such as paying someone to come into your house to care for you, or paying your medical bills. Overall, this person has the broadest authority to make decisions on your behalf while you're alive.

Protecting Minor And Young Adult Children

There are two vital steps for parents to take to protect their children, especially when their children are still under 18 years of age. These two actions are:

1. Naming a guardian for their children in their will. This only applies to minor children and provides someone to care for them in case both parents die.
2. Setting up a trust and naming a trustee to manage the funds until the children can inherit them. This is especially important for minors, but can apply to children of any age, even adult children.

Powers Of Attorney For Your Adult Children

As far as protecting children in other capacities, such as making sure they have power of attorney, the parent has the authority to do things on their child's behalf until they reach 18. Once the child reaches 18 years of age, they could give their parents power of attorney or name them as health care proxy, if they choose.

When a young adult is in college, the parent can't automatically find everything out unless they've been given the power of attorney. It comes as a shock to parents when they can't get medical information about their 19-year-old, especially if it's something urgent.

With their parent is their power of attorney, if the child is in the hospital for some reason, the parent can find out everything they need to know about the medical situation. They can talk to doctors and look at medical records, which they cannot do without the power of attorney.

While not as common, it is still possible for a young person or college student to need an advance directive, such as if they fall into a coma or become brain-dead after a tragic accident. In cases like this, there is often confusion about whether this person should be on life support or not. If the child's parents are divorced, this can create even more tension and complications.

In a perfect world, the person heading off to college would do an advance directive. They can state their wishes and name a decision maker, who would likely be mom, or dad, or both. Even if your child is no longer legally a minor, there are still ways you can protect them. If you have a young adult child, you may want to speak to them about naming you or their other parent as their power of attorney or health care proxy.

CHAPTER 8

ADULT GUARDIANSHIPS

The Process For Obtaining An Adult Guardianship

Adult guardianships typically occur when someone has not appointed a power of attorney, so they have no decision maker. When someone becomes mentally incapacitated, such as with cases of advanced dementia, they need a decision maker.

A lawyer can prepare a complaint to be filed on behalf of someone who cares for the mentally incapacitated person. The complaint generally describes the person's situation, states their assets, and provides medical documentation.

Then, at least two doctors must examine the ward, (the person who is mentally incapacitated), and come to the conclusion that the person is unable to manage their personal and financial affairs.

The judge or the court will then appoint a lawyer to represent the alleged incapacitated person to make sure their interests are protected. This is because the guardian becomes the person's decision maker for everything, and it takes away that person's liberty completely.

The Role Of An Adult Guardian

So what does a guardian do? A guardian's role is similar to that of a power of attorney. They pay the person's bills, make decisions about their assets, decide what nursing home or assisted living the person should go to, and more…

The authority of a guardian is very broad. They can't make a will for the person, but they can do pretty much anything else. They are responsible for all kinds of medical decision-making, including life-or-death situations.

Additionally, a guardian can make decisions on behalf of their ward about:

- Whether they should live or die, if they are in an end-of-life scenario;
- Whether a piece of real estate they own should be sold;
- What in-home care agency to use, and how much to pay them;
- And much more…

Because the court wants to make sure that the guardian is doing their job properly, the guardian is usually required to report annually to the court about how the ward is doing. Sometimes, they have to file an accounting document that shows what actions they've taken, and what monies come into or leave the ward's financial accounts.

When An Adult Guardianship Is Needed

The difference between a conservator and a guardian is basically that a conservator is limited to making financial decisions, whereas a guardian makes financial, medical, and other decisions. Obtaining guardianship is a court process that usually takes around two to four months. Since it is a very involved process, this is another great reason to do a power of attorney while you are well.

Guardianships are never needed unless someone has not completed a power of attorney. Typically, if you've executed an advance directive, you would've also elected a power of attorney, which means there would be no need for a guardianship.

Usually, a guardian is appointed for someone that also doesn't have an advance directive, though occasionally, our firm does see applications to have a guardian appointed where there is an advance directive in place.

When this happens, the court will often nullify the advance directive for health care, because you can't have two people as the decision makers. For this reason, the court places all the decision-making with the guardian.

In a court proceeding, when there is an advance directive with a person named, the proposed guardian would have to put that person on notice. The person named in the advance directive would come to court, and they could object to the guardianship. In that kind of scenario, the court might just limit the guardian to non-medical decision-making, and keep the health care proxy in place.

The options are generally that either the health care proxy is revoked by the court, or they separate the decision-making. However, leaving the health care proxy to make medical decisions while the guardian makes financial ones is rare.

CHAPTER 9

ADDITIONAL ADVANTAGES OF ESTATE PLANNING

In-Life Benefits Of Estate Planning

While most people think of estate planning as something that's only useful after their passing, some of the documents can be necessary and profoundly helpful during someone's lifetime...

A will is only consequential after the person has passed. Creating a Will for in-life benefits is not legal or effective.

However, while not always utilized, the other two basic estate planning documents - the power of attorney and advance directive - can be extremely beneficial in a person's lifetime.

The power of attorney is probably the most important lifetime estate planning document you can have. This person can do business for you - talk to people, withdraw money, sell stocks, sell real estate, and much more. A power of attorney may never do anything for you, or they might have a 20-year job, depending on the circumstances.

The advance directive, while not always used, can also help you during a lifetime. In extreme cases where you are living only artificially (with the support of machines, etc.), then the advance directive can help you because it states your wishes about your treatment.

Keeping Your Loved Ones Out Of Court

Although there are no guarantees, proper estate planning definitely makes it much more likely that your loved ones will stay out of court. This is because your wishes are clearly stated and there should be no disputes.

What's more, when you state in your will who exactly is inheriting your assets and who your executor will be, there is no argument about who the executor should be or who should inherit your affairs.

Estate Taxes

As of 2018, there are no more estate taxes in New Jersey. There is still an inheritance tax in New Jersey, but that usually only impacts cases where assets have been left to people who are not a person's kids or grandkids. The estate tax that was based on value is gone, which means it is no longer necessary to give away assets to minimize estate tax – at least in New Jersey.

There is still a federal estate tax, but it doesn't affect a lot of people because you are generally allowed $12 million per person ($24 million per couple) free of federal estate tax. For those with significant assets above that threshold, there are tools we can use to minimize these taxes.

For example, we can create credit shelter trusts in both spouses' wills. This allows the first spouse who passes away to leave some of their money to a credit shelter trust, rather than leaving it all for their surviving spouse. Then, when the surviving spouse pass away, the assets in the credit shelter trust would pass to their kids, free of federal estate tax.

CHAPTER 10

PROBATE

An Overview Of Probate

Generally, probate refers to the process by which a person's assets are distributed after their death, whether they die with or without a will. Different states have different complexity levels for the probate process.

In New Jersey, probate involves going to the surrogate's office. The surrogate is a judge who works in an office setting rather than a courtroom, and who is in charge of all estates.

After someone's passing, you bring the original will and death certificate to the surrogate's office, and as long as there are two witnesses and a notary, then the will is probated. Probate just means validation of a will, if the will is done correctly.

Probate Disputes

Probate issues usually arise when a parent has treated the kids unequally or disinherited one of them. When disputes occur, it slows down the probate process significantly.

One of the kids might think they should have benefited, and they may file a lawsuit. They may claim that the person who made the will was subject to "undue influence." A typical scenario where this could occur is when one of the children still lives with that parent, or is their caretaker.

For example, let's look at a scenario where a mother has three kids; one lives with her, and the other two live out of state. When their mother passes, she leaves everything to the caregiver child and cuts out the other two, or only gives them a little bit.

In these cases, there may be an allegation that the live-in child took advantage of their mother's frailty and lack of judgment, or that he convinced her to leave everything to them as the caregiver. Sometimes these kinds of allegations are accurate, and sometimes they are not.

In any case, these situations occur more often when the parent is totally dependent on their child for medical care. This child does everything for their parent, and is in a position to unduly influence or substitute their judgment for her mom's independent judgment. This can cause the parent, either against their will or not, to create a will that leaves out the other children.

There are several potential outcomes for this type of situation. First of all, the will could be set aside.

Or, if the other siblings could prove undue influence, then they would receive some portion of the estate. If they're successful, they usually receive more of the estate than the will says they were entitled to receive.

Hiring A Probate Litigation Attorney

Typically, when you are served with a complaint, that is when you should hire a probate attorney.

If a will is challenged, the executor is the person that gets sued, even if they are not the person that is being accused of undue influence. The executor needs to hire a probate litigation lawyer, as they are the one the lawsuit is filed against.

The executor's fees are paid from the estate, so there is no need for them to pay out of pocket for attorney fees.

If you're a beneficiary and you believe that you have a legitimate basis to challenge a will, then you would want to hire a probate litigation attorney to see if there was undue influence.

Alternatively, the person may have been mentally incapacitated when they wrote the will, and they shouldn't have written one. If this is the case, it is possible that someone made sure they did, which is also undue influence.

CHAPTER 11

THE DIFFERENCE THE RIGHT FIRM MAKES

The Importance Of Working With The Right Lawyer

Estate planning and probate are not things you want to handle on your own. Some of the litigation I've handled in the past was the result of a person going online and trying to do their own estate planning. One situation comes to mind of a case where someone's cousin printed out a legal will form for them. Their cousin had them sign it, and of course, there were problems with the will, not to mention that the cousin received the entire estate, to the exclusion of all others.

This also led to allegations of undue influence against the cousin, because she basically created the will. Instead of taking the person to a lawyer, she printed it from the internet, and she got the woman to sign it, along with two witnesses and a notary.

When I work with clients, I don't meet with their beneficiaries. If I'm working with a couple who has kids, I don't meet with the kids. If someone were to write a will that favors someone who was brought into my office, that could cause problems for the attorney, the clients, and their beneficiaries.

In short, if you're not using a lawyer to do a will, it can result in litigation. No matter what your goals may be, it's essential to work with a professional lawyer who is experienced with estate planning.

What Sets Our Firm Apart

Some lawyers or law firms view estate planning as if it were an unwanted stepchild. They'll deal with it when the client wants them to - but it's not really what they want to do, nor do they enjoy it - so they'll only do the bare minimum.

If you go to a lawyer that's not serious about estate planning - maybe they specialize in litigation, so they're in court all the time and they're busy - so they just pump out a standard form will. They don't take the time to get to know their client and find out what their specific needs might be and they might not even create a power of attorney or advance directive. That's simply wrong.

But if you've gotten this far into the book, you can easily see how that's a huge problem.

As for our firm, estate planning is what we do. Wills, powers of attorney, advance directives, and estate administration: at least 80% of my legal practice has something to do with estates, whether it's planning, probate, or litigation.

I'm known in this area for being a trusts and estates lawyer. People have a tendency to think of me when they think of a T&E lawyer because I've presented myself in that way over the years, have many clients in that area, and provided seminars to the public and other lawyers as to trust and estate issues.

It's important for clients to hire someone who takes trust and estate planning seriously, and that is what we do. We're comprehensive about it: we ask the right questions, we prepare the right documents, and we send them to you to take a look at. If changes are needed, we change things.

We also are prepared to go out of our way for clients. Of course, people usually come into our office, but if someone needs us to go to a hospital or a nursing home, we'll go to them if they can't come to us.

The biggest thing is we don't view estate planning as an orphan. We view it as the essential thing that it is. We know that estate planning can have serious, significant impacts on people's lives, and we don't take that for granted. We understand that. We appreciate that. That's why estate planning is our focus, and that's why we have done it consistently for 19 years.

What Is The Next Step?

For assistance with your estate law matter, please feel free to contact us by e-mail or phone at 908.232.0099. We reply to all phone calls and e-mails promptly, usually within the same day.

Index

A

advance directive · 31
advanced dementia · 30

B

beneficiaries · 28

C

caregiver · 71
cerebral palsy · 35
certificates of deposits (CDs) · 47
co-administrators · 23
common misconceptions · 19
conservator · 63
credit shelter trust · 68

D

death certificate · 70

E

end-of-life care and treatment · 56
estate administrator · 23
estate planning · 26
estate planning documents · 45
estate plans · 33
estate representative · 25
executor · 21

F

federal estate tax · 67

G

guardianship · 30

H

health care proxy · 33

I

inheritance tax · 67

L

legal decision-maker · 30
letter of testamentary · 21
living trust · 19

M

Medicaid · 35
medical decision-making · 62
medical documentation · 61
mentally incapacitated · 29

P

payable-on-death beneficiary · 47
payable-on-death designation · 47
power of attorney (POA) · 28
probate · 74
probate litigation attorney · 72
probate process · 69

S

special needs · 35
SSI · 35
surrogate · 69
surviving joint account owner · 49

T

testator · 39

trustees · 43

W

will · 22

NOTES

Made in United States
Troutdale, OR
11/03/2026

56844898R00052